Midwest Hymns

Midwest Hymns

Poems by

Dale Cottingham

Cover design by Shay Culligan
Cover photograph from Getty Images

ISBN: 978-1-63980-234-0

Kelsay Books
502 South 1040 East, A-119
American Fork, Utah 84003
Kelsaybooks.com

The poems in this volume are dedicated to David, Ava, Joe,
and Holly, who each knew what it was like,
and not forgetting Leon and Donald, both passing too soon,
and Susan, who saw me through.

Acknowledgments

Grateful acknowledgment is made to the editors of the journals that first published the following poems, sometimes in earlier versions:

Asheville Poetry Review: "Photo of My Father, Kansas City, 1946"

Brevities: "Grandfather's Ground," "Measure," "Night Calling," "West of Alva, Oklahoma"

Eunoia Review: "Family Time"

Ibbetson Street: "Blaine County Uplift Nights," "In the Kitchen," "Pole Barn," "Pond Gone Dry"

Literary Nest: "Swan Dive"

Main Street Rag: "Rural Funeral"

Midwest Review: "A Moral Life" (finalist in the 2021 Great Midwest Writing Contest)

Ploughshares: "No One's Fault"

Poetry Depth Quarterly: "After the Wind Shift"

Sow's Ear: "Reach"

Contents

III

IV

I

History Once Removed

Roll's one-room schoolhouse
is not in Roll anymore.
The county took it
to a lawn of mowed Bermuda
at the fairgrounds,
painting its clapboard
a sturdy citizen white,
renewing the roof
with hand-cut shakes
aping a freshly minted
suburban home—shutters
once fallen to rickety ruin restored,
replacing panes blinded
by bored boys pitching
beer bottles on Friday nights,
or shot by hunters
returning home short of prey.
Now the view inside
exposes an unlit, empty room,
where generations
of farm children
read American classics:
Moby Dick, Walden, Poe,
their feet restless
on that hard wood floor
with some brightness
or shadowed terror
the language revealed.

No One's Fault

It wasn't her fault: she fell running
across the open space.

Knee bleeding, she wouldn't
get picked for the team.

None of us understood, of course:
we had no word for this.

I've read that on Earth our breath
is as soughing, that we are not our own

deliverance, which seems right after all.
What she did was unbutton her cotton dress

facing us, unbidden, in her white panties
inventing the strangeness of the other in our eyes.

Pond Gone Dry

Beyond the roadside fence, some rancher's
pushed up an earthen embankment
for a pond gone dry.

Maybe the snowmelt
and rain runoff
are too meager to fill it—

or maybe the dam's soil
is too porous, too poor,
to hold what it receives.

Maybe the rains haven't
come right for too long,
exposing tangled weeds and silt.

It's like this on these plains,
some ideas thrown up in hope
over time, that fail to take.

Learning to Swim

Stripped to my underwear,
Dad in jeans, no shirt,
we wade so far out
on the sandy lake bottom
that the assurance
of anything firm to stand on
is beyond my tiptoes—my face
below water—I must push off
to top the surface for
a hurried breath of inland air.
My eyes are roving appetites
that want to see, then see some more.
Sometimes I get to look on my own.
But today, Dad points the way
to feeling, tossing me into the deeps.
When I bob up looking for him,
he shouts, *Swim out!*
I windmill my arms and legs, flailing,
for all I am worth.

Killdeer

No bigger, and no more
ferocious than a child's fist,
camouflaged survivor

of every weather, I cannot
get close enough
to know her scent,

though I suspect
the rich aroma
of native soil with its

hint of tartness,
terrestrial as she is,
wings unable to fly,

bound to the floor
of these plains.
Her lithe legs

no bigger than pipe cleaners,
made for running
in bursts,

a frenzy of motion,
as she twigs over
plowed ground.

She watches me
with oversized dark eyes
that scrutinize my every movement.

Most days I keep a trustworthy distance,
but this morning,
spotting her nest,

a useful construction
of native grass, a bit of debris,
a small woven cup

of a home on the ground,
I see two brown-speckled,
cappuccino-colored eggs,

holding a future untold.
When I step closer
to get a better look,

her small voice shrills
alarm in June air, and she runs,
dipping, swerving in circles

away from her nest,
holding out one wing,
feigning injury,

creating a diversion
to distract me from her nest
exposed on the open ground.

Two Trees

Harbored from north winds
by the barn, two trees grew

together, close as lovers:
decades wove their limbs, so one's

branch bore the other's leaves—
till a hard freeze

reached the heartwood,
rendering the roots useless.

Come spring, one tree
wore luminous green,

pungent leaves breathing
April's warmer air

while the other
stayed a lifeless gray,

as if one died
in the arms of the other.

In the Kitchen

The sprawling chairs belie my pinched appearance,
conversation stalling in our mouths,
we kickstart like a balky appliance.
Memory reminds me I once took pleasure
in your graceful apple paring—

now the cupboard we chose,
paid too much for, sits in a corner
we no longer see, storing sorrow and shame.

We chat without conviction
of taking an Italian vacation,
missing accidental happiness
we found in the kitchen,
when evening sifted through the open window,
and words seemed beside the point—

my breath misting your hair,
the turn of your head as you felt it—
the smile on your upturned face.

Family Photo

We stand in front of the porch
dressed in T-shirts, jeans, some in boots,
as straight for the lens as each can manage.
I am held by a cousin, Jack,
who'd return from Vietnam a decade later a recluse,
who is next to Bruce, disappeared,
also a decade later, turning up as a waiter in New Orleans
after exiling himself to Canada
to avoid the draft, next to Paul,
a backhoe operator who'd die of heart failure, in 2013.
None of us knew any of this was coming,
or that the infant, one of the twenty-two relations pictured,
would be borne into a vast plain
of words, searching its grasses for seeds in chaff,
while fate ticks off his remaining minutes.

Grandfather's Ground

Do the rains still refuse to fall?
Can you still plow in the way
you taught yourself, but not your boys,
to draw up moisture from the ground?

On land just off the Petite Jean,
the year 1932, the crop
that almost, but did not,
fail.

After the Wind Shift

How cool the air! From the glowing fields,
wheat like tiny hands reaching skyward,
as they must, in silence, in morning sun, the road
dividing the sighing grasses, with a supple bend.

Standing beside me, your keen face
brightening, wearing your cotton shift—white,
breezy as our conversation. Dew on the grass,
and a clear, level light, gracing the early hour.

Small Flatland Town

In lieu of more pavement's
easy travel, a gravel road
whose baked stones cool
as dusk eases the heat.

A man tamps a last post
into hardpan he chipped a hole in,
as two boys on one bike
unsettle a flock of starlings
perched on the high wire.

A young woman at her sink
thinks of a word she thought
she'd lost, then
writes it down.

At the church amongst
the small congregation of houses,
untrained voices raise
a hymn in the evening air,
while two dogs lying
amicably on a lawn
raise their heads
and join the chorus,
singing the darkness in.

Blaine County Uplift Nights

As night shades the flat squared land below,
isolate farm lights guide returning
men and women, who wash their hands
and share a meal in worn, familiar clothes.

As work etches their palm lines deeper,
I like to think some are writing poems
at scarred kitchen tables, tired from doing
all that could be done that day, but not
too tired to attempt what may be.

Watching from tonight's moonless depths,
lit only by starlight exhausted from traveling
the great emptiness out there to no fullness here—
no instructions or divine hand to guide mine,
today's light already gone, tomorrow's yet to pass by.

Family Time

We thought we'd mastered it,
those breezy gerunds, gust fronts
from adverbial phrases,
minor winds from indirect objects
we passed around after dinner like pie.
But, little darlings, don't we find ways
to fill the empty middle ground
and tell our silly selves
what we like to hear and call it meaning?
The space gets filled.
We even look back and say
it seemed like a dream,
but we were there all the time,
in body, sometimes even in mind.
Doesn't the family make you feel like a cry?
That, too, will pass, like so much:
the rituals we made parting,
the prayers we said—if only I had meant them.
You must remember the November night
I visited you in the family room,
your cable TV uncharacteristically off,
as I asked how the war years were for you.
Blurting a truth I never knew, you offered
that you held a letter in your first wife's script
reading *pregnant, divorce,* as you teetered anew
in a gust on the cliff.

II

Pole Barn

In it we stored what was useful
or what we couldn't bear
to let go of altogether, settling
by letting go as far as the barn.

Willed into place, Shaker-simple,
three rows of three great poles,
girth wide as a man, shouldered up
and set down in hand-dug holes,

corrugated steel panels for walls,
and for roof, nailed in with ribbed nails,
two-by-fours serving as joists,
rising like a dream all summer.

A sanctum where I lingered, inhaling its smell
of dry dirt floor and solvent, dust
suspended in darkened air, to fetch
an awl or ax or whatever I was sent for,

until it was taken by fire, the flames
overwhelming our hose
and spreading over the structure,
volumes of black smoke rising:

a harvest of what fomented when I'd sit
watching haying across the road,
the machine's intake, the right, square bales,
gone to heat, weeds, stubble, dust.

Fence

I

Beyond the roadside's sidling ditch,
I parallel a rancher's fence:

four strands pulled to metal poles. I walk
the gravel road as May sun reaches zenith—

no one sees me beneath low clouds
blown by wind whose earth tang promises rain.

The fence marks a boundary
bespeaking a human fear,

but from what I can see, the sun, wind,
rain pay no attention.

II

When I round the far side of the curve,
I see a downed section of fence,

wire draping posts lying in dust,
a human claim staked and lost.

I know there's a time and place
for keeping things in, or out,

but with no effort, I could step
between wires beyond fear or pride

to walk the land's
higher reaches,

or rummage gullies
new to me.

Under a cloudless sky
in the middle of treeless hills,

in sight of no eyes, I smiled,
for what had been let go,

loosening a tightness in my chest,
and deepening my breathing.

Night Calling

Late one night, I paused
a restless moment on the porch,
long after the sun's final light,

and heard from nearby sycamores
an owl's black velvet question
like a hymn sung by heart,

but more lonesome,
a hollow solo in minor key
that seemed to speak for me

as I looked into that night,
as the south wind stroked my face
like a lover's ghost,

as a cloud curtained
the half-moon and moved on,
as if it finished its mission—

and after a long time
(was it?) from far down the swale
came a matching reply.

Kitchen Door

Mine's a stodgy wooden creaks-
when-you-move-it affair,
an uncurtained, chest-high
window, square in the middle,
to help me see where I'm going:
the steps, backyard, shed.
Yes, it's farmhouse white,
highlighting the yellowed field
of stains around the knob made
by all the oblivious passers-through.
It's more intimate than the front door's
formal face, shown
to unexpected callers or relatives
unseen since Christmas. It makes
no judgments that linger
like whispered reputations
from lip to ear. It has no memory
of a teenager's missed curfew,
adjusting clothing and hair
in case someone waited up.
No memory of a man's despair,
admitting the shame of what
he'd become aloud. It accepts
and allows, its easy swinging
makes each morning fresh,
like a saint who keeps loving
no matter what sins are committed here.

Gone

The old fishing rod and reel
lie on the dollar table
at the garage sale
like a lost thought.
One metal eye is missing,
another two have gone wrong,
the fiberglass shaft
has lost its sheen,
dull as a dried-out reed
on the bank of a pond.
The open-faced reel grins
like an old man,
for no reason we can see,
the filament as tangled
as an out-of-order mind.
Gone are the days
when it rested on a nail
in the shed, ready
to be taken in hand. Gone
are the nights it lay
on the edge of an inland lake,
its filament threading
the far dark silty water,
in hope of some drama,
a slack line pulled
good and tight enough
for the man looking back
on innocence
he never thought he'd miss.

Driving into Canadian County

As we drive, and the earth turns red,
as if to answer an artist's wish,
you say it wasn't sorrow you felt

when you reached across the blank field
of sheets to your then-wife, who stiffened
her legs like iron gates rusted shut,

but an electric leap your mind made to Miłosz,
who wrote, the way you remembered it,
that, in leaving our lives, we salvage
no more than a few words
from all our reading, speaking, and breathing—

we drive in silence for miles,
in afternoon light fiery enough
to have burned the earth red
in the distance we head into,
as the land we've known goes by.

Digging Postholes in Hardpan

I found it packed so tight,
that when I stabbed it with the posthole digger,
it chipped no letter off, much less a word.

I poured water from the battered plastic pail,
while the implacable red ground taunted me
with my weakness, threatening failure,

I chipped and hammered the first hole
in a hard-won line of holes, blisters
forming on my ten-year-old hands,

but I was learning that June to savor
morning's cool allowance
against heat destined to oppress the rest of the day.

West of Alva, Oklahoma

Farther on, the land opens up
to grassy plains.
No mountains, no trees,
no dramatic precipice edging
hairpin curves.

Only this monotonous,
unremarkable, flat expanse,
like a man who's given up
every pretense he used to own.

Plunging Ahead

A swarthy wind muscles me
toward the easier way,
where the land unwrinkles,
but I take the other, hilly, less kind,
because it's more like what I've known.

I plunge into a gully,
all elbows and clammy breathing,
spongy bottom underfoot,
I look up from the place
where soil once was—
the in-between, the underneath,
the very ground of poetry.

Making a Way Home

As I drive away, tall grass stalks sway
in wind gusts, billowing like waves,
but rooted in resistance, springing up
when the wind finally dies.

Why shouldn't we take our cues
from what's given, since nothing
will take its place, why not dance our way
to the void, in case no heaven awaits?

Returning to your place,
we drive through sleet, pellets
pelting the windshield like artillery,
ice glazing trees like witnesses to glory.
They said the storm might do this,
but no one could say for sure.
While we're both still whole,
it's time to make up a way home.

III

Straightening Nails

A riot's aftermath, silvered shanks
rigored in generous curves or nearly perfect
fishhooks of fetal dreamers,

all of them bent from the pry bar
that wrenched them from the home
they'd been hammered into.

We cannot know their precise stories,
though the lengths suggest a handful
held in anonymity, a dining-room wall,

perhaps our own, hosting yearly Thanksgivings,
the lingering pecan pie flavor punctuating
whatever fullness we reached that season—

or a bedroom where two tried
to lose themselves in each other's hunger—
while other, stubbier nails tacked shingles

to roofs to keep out weather
allowing life to unfold unabated.
I touch a pair to my tongue:

one tastes stainless-steel clean,
the other of rust and ruin,
but equal in tensile strength.

The coffee can of nails preserved through
winter freezes and summer thunderstorms,
I take from an outbuilding shelf

to a flat rock in shade, where I place
the chosen one between forefinger and thumb,
raising a hammer with the other hand,

tamping slowly at first,
straightening its crooked past,
not made new, but newly useful.

Recovery Ward

Why do I miss that lumpy
pull-out couch? I never asked
its origin in the roomscape
or what music you heard
in your mind when you woke.
In this careless way, we let
what happened happen, bleaching out
the fabric we'd woven between us,
and haven't seen each other since.

Now, it's All Saints Day. Evening
routs sun earlier than wont,
as the yellowing trees whisper
their liturgy, a history told
in spade-shaped leaves.
I spent the lunar year regretting
my ambulance adventures,
whose sirens lull me to sleep,
to dream a brighter moon, still feeling
the curve of the myth you lent.

2 AM

I've been told it's the hour of salvation.
I wake like a stepped-on rake,
glazed, but electric as a fence,
as wind shivers the eaves.

Only moments ago I dreamed
faces I once knew, scenes
vaguely familiar: a corridor
swirling in silvered red, green,
like ballgowns from a bygone time.

Now, I'm shed of everything
save my blurry eyes, shallow breath.

Conduit

Dad, you never asked me,
but I never considered objecting.

Mostly, I didn't pay attention,
which meant I was cared for—

which I took for granted.
Still, you took me with you

on your mission to the nursing home,
where, unfazed by the unmuted urine odor,

you laid out cup, brush, and razor, then tipped
each veteran's frail face for a shave,

you, who dug your face into the sand at Iwo,
who gave yourself over to others' hands

and came back changed: a conduit
for temporary states of grace.

Rural Funeral

Organ music swells around us,
as we sit lucid and still.

The bright afternoon festers
with August heat, fields rest blankly,
farmhouses stand isolate
and stir a little.

Cars scour the gravel road, kick up dust.
Somewhere mail is delivered.
Somewhere a woman looks over land she's known
and wonders where else she could be.

The stunned family gathers in pews
near the casket, each and all of us
taking what comes, just as the low hills
take what comes. The church,
its pine appurtenances, the worn
carpet, deep red, is thick with us,

as we sit lucid and still.

The young husband of the dead
doesn't know what to do with his grief.
He bends forward,

arms crossed over his body,
humming,
lost in a song that she sang.

Mid-Continent

If I stood naked under my clothes, I wasn't alone.
I applauded Einstein's theories.
I lived in the shadow of Oppenheimer's project.
I've not taken the road I'm on all the way to the sea.
When I was born, trucks sped on cheap gasoline,
and the music of their wheels,
whining like steel guitars, ran like a river,
through plains cut into parts—some, like mine,
inhabited by veterans of war and depression.
Too far to walk, we drove cars to buy groceries,
jeans, and magazines in town, where movies
were parceled out to us from the far, exotic Hollywood,
and television said we were going to the moon.
Schools remained open. Opinions spread like fever.
The plough was put to the ground.

Roadside Dump

Here, in the center of immensity,
it seems an afterthought,
my derelict collection, one signpost

on my morning walk, substance
of a composition made more ludicrous
by sunlight, and vast, over low hills,

this June morning wind,
heavy with moisture portending rain—
a roadside dump the size of a two-room cottage.

I study the bewildering intricacy of sloth
with new eyes, the heap spent, broken,
dirt-covered, yet vaguely luminous,

like pages in an album
of scenes you've forgotten in a closet,
an entire aesthetic of failure: the child's bike

surely once shimmered in a garage, treasured,
ridden in the Fourth of July parade,
whose bent front wheel makes

a permanent three-quarters moon, spokes
protruding like pins in air; a ripped trash bag
revealing a collage of shirts and dresses,

here morello, the color of dewberries,
there a green fading to yellow,
like leaves exhausted by August.

Nearest to me, a toy truck,
peeping optimistically from the heap,
despite its crushed bed,

like a dream I wake from shaking.
Through its encrusted dirt, I read
the industrial stamp, *Taiwan,* a detail

I would have missed
before art taught me
to focus on the *all* around me—

wind swimming through grass billowing
like waves, or layered sand, rock, clay,
the rigid and brittle interlaced with the giving,

exposed by the road cut, revealing a history I walk on,
or dust suspended on a windless August evening,
glinting, gleaming, levitating over a field.

Attention finds mystery and beauty enough
for any mortal, even in the mid-continent,
a flyover place for many, lacking great cities

and mountain vistas, offering only these
low and lower undulations, hills and grasses,
where I see a vast page awaiting art,

poetry in the dazzling morning haze,
and in mounding debris,
where a lexicon of desire and loss

may be shoved out the back of a pickup
some summer night, lightening a load,
and'making history, anthropological strata

my road cuts through this morning
under expanding light, sun glancing off
dewy grass, off the dump like jewels,

reflected, refracted—gleaming browns,
mauves, a multitude of skin colors, a result
of chance or destiny, either way, a fabulous disarray.

Photo of My Father, Kansas City, 1946

The sun shines on him as he walks,
his face lit with his future,
the narrow storefront's
glass reflecting his back
like an opened door.
The deep Pacific,
the ship's pitch and roll
from silent currents
in the unfathomed sea
that mark his stance
are not before him anymore,
nor the Petite Jean farm's mean hopes.

I wonder who took the photo—
a woman lost to memory?
I never asked. He never said. Such
are the borders between fathers and sons,
of the unspoken.

We are told the poem must show,
not say, and I sometimes believe that—

show me the path, the gate—
show me how it opens.

Close-Up

I thought I knew more
in my youth than I do now.

I've regressed or accepted
so much, I've taken

to reading *Dilbert,*
whose head looks

like a smokestack
about to blow.

He stays contained
by keeping to-do lists

of the mundane,
of every task

best done alone,
crunching mute numbers

programmed to obey.
Strangely enough,

my love calls
in the middle

of today's new strip,
surely portending

thunder in the bushes,
humorous negotiations

in the furthest reaches
of the garden—

claims will be adjusted,
with choices between

delicious alternatives.
I'll hover near the bed,

awaiting a signal
from an accountant—

or priest—
as if this were the end

of the fiscal year.

Reach

He stands at the porch rail
in overalls worn thin,
shouting, *Caw! Caw! Caw!*,
his Adam's apple bobbing
like a cork, calling to real crows
in the band of trees
lining the far edge of the yard. Gone,
the days he walked
fence lines, finding
downed wires to fix.

Gone, the times
he stayed up late,
hunched over
the kitchen table,
figuring the fuel bill,
next month's groceries,
gripping the pencil nub
in the small circle of light
where he worked.

Gone are the nights he lay
in the plain's immense darkness,
listening to his pulse.
Now, he strains at the rail,
leaning into each caw,
his falsetto spiraling
over the yard, like a promise
he intends to keep.

IV

Disassembly

I

Our colloquy ended in June,
under coursing wind. An intrusion
flooded my face like an immersion
in an iron order that spread like rust
from the mind's back lots, and created
in its stilted lurch a fated saneness:
vagaries took you too soon.
Not that the wind took notice
as it toiled in ditches,
threading grass, roadside debris.

As autumn deepens, the question sharpens:
whether I'll dare further over open ground
exposing my face, up, then downslope,
past contemplation of a solitary grass blade, the self
alone, bending to vagrant winds.
My movement, no longer real to you,
for me is a world entire. On back roads,
I find new options in conditions,
observing what got tossed,
reaching feelers into afternoon's long shadows,
blown clouds: what I draw in like sustaining breath.

From outside, my breath mingles lightly
with surrounding air,
disturbing nothing visible,
while evening slips on robes of night,
but, inside, it wrenches words, images,
as I extract what I can from now-silvered events.
I still hear familiar sounds: traffic,

talk from the next booth, wind
moaning in high wires voicing what I've felt,
sounds I see as symbols,
marking an unmarked path.

II

Walking further, I shuck extraneous keys,
yield my desire to win through.
Not caring what fashion I wear, unaware
of the day of the week,
I focus on what's underfoot.
Emboldened in this faithful way,
I try on ideas that prism in plain light
into greens, deep purples, swirls of red,
while a fidelity I once thought serious,
becomes a kind of play.

That play coalesces in a hollow,
where in a rumpus-room atmosphere,
the structures I've made disassemble,
like glints off breaking crystal.
When the fog lifts for a moment,
adjectives glitter, commas pile on,
trees rise to give shade: a time without time.
Descending sun still paints evening,
trees lean in wind,
clouds pass over land only appearing
to waver.

I suspect others feel this, too, revealed
by daydreaming looks from back stoops
at trackless landscapes shaped by rain, heat,

by winter's freeze. But daily quandaries,
bills, evening meals, grind this to powder.
We found a way to share our rights,
but not our goods. The great flower
of what we could have been, stunted
by a dirt road's dust,
by isolating fences where we live
destined to solitude, to private consolations.

III

In this landscape, I ambulate curves
of small roles I played. Flirting with the girl
in the blue one-piece, watching a storm
gather humid air, summer heat,
whatever's within reach, rising
like an intellect to rage over innocent land.
My self-imposed task is to examine that ground,
view sun flecks on rock, imagine
dust raising an aura in midafternoon,
a vocabulary for appraising distance.

Like rain, you exist only in falling,
sometimes soothing heat-stunned leaves,
but also forging torrents, gathering force,
further eroding the cut bank, exposing
my layered soil, disassembling my gathered debris.
My wish for you was never more ample
than the flamboyant clothes you wore
or what you faced in the volcanic antechamber:
the guy you picked up, brought home,
calling me later to say how trashy it was.

Your livid voice punctuated my ankle-weighted
plodding, predictable as a syllabus,
confirming breath as the ghost
in my machine I greet each morning,
and lose track of after the horizon's fixed poles
have faded into night.
Enthralled by tree shadows dividing light,
by every stone underfoot,
smaller, freer, I take the open way,
more like my original intent.

IV

Last summer came careless
as girls splashing at the lake,
with hints of the other seasons:
autumn, the man in a corduroy suit.
Spring, the child running in high wind.
Winter, the jacketed soldier
parading a narrow path.
They said you rested without pain,
no doubt confined to a room too small
for your vast imagination,
your lessons unraveling
in stillness that would not bear you
to the ravine's other side.
Surely, in that last flicker,
you whispered a secret to yourself.

After every kind of disassembly,
I am left with this self
scored by lilts, by tones overheard.

You and I once marked each other with glyphs
exposed in open air, which means—
and this is lovely—
amid the chaos we're given to each other,
we are not alone.
During hard nights under winter's advance,
I'll remember that bright inkling,
and give thanks for words
of salving grace that look at first like loss.

Measure

One Sunday, while most were sleeping in,
I saw in the interstate median
a mule deer, glossy and muscular,
galloping along a concrete retaining wall
trying to find escape.
No other travelers shared
that moment, stopping
to attempt aid or photographs,
as the wind combed his burled fur,
but when I drove past,
close enough to meet his gaze,
his dark eyes held a fierceness,
that in that instant took my measure,
more than any human look I've known.

Glass of Well Water

When I pour it, the silver stream
twines through abiding air
sounding like laughter in the glass
I fill half-full, or half-empty,
so lithe today is my point of view.
I've carried water from this well
in a plastic pail to nurse fruit trees
oppressed by summer drought,
to wash my face and neck,
sweat-stained and dirty
from hoeing or digging postholes,
but now I quench a thirst no labor's earned,
tasting chalk, yet tart as memory,
dredged from underground,
where water's held in darkness, in silence,
till it fills this glass, and sets
my parched mouth free to speak.

Guaranteed In-Garage Shelter

As lightning throws its jagged spears
from cloud to ground, and thunder

barrels down the street, my mother
turns on news, watching the helicopter view

of the great cloud lowering, the meteorologist
drawing a course toward her.

Still in her cotton housecoat,
she goes to the garage, and slides

the armored door, stepping
into a cup of safety not much bigger

than a grave. Such resorts wait
all over town, places to meditate,

while winds howl with divine fury,
deciding what to raze. She emerges

in the aftermath, face upturned,
laboring less climbing up stairs

than down, buoyed
into one more afterlife.

Sunset at Boise City

Two boys out after supper
shoot the last hoops they can see,
as pale light shortens the streets,
and a man eases into his driveway—
old and young both wondering
if another world exists beyond this,
beyond surrounding short grass hills,
where they'll one day find themselves.
The dogs turn thrice around
before settling down,
boys make the most of the day's last light,
and old men are content
to let darkness in.

In the Examination Room

My brother and I hold him up
to the scales, both sons
middle-aged, each bearing half
his frail weight, whose measure
will provide useless information
to the waiting nurse, ready
with digital tablet to record
what regulations say are vital.
The wall in front of him says
he won't go much farther,
while his frail gown
waves senselessly at the floor.
At what must have seemed
to him a high step,
he rises with two missing discs,
determined to complete his assignment.
What grace he owns
shows in his face, looking
as he best can from his stoop,
to whatever the future holds.
We three are the ones
who dug postholes in hard clay
one windswept June, looked
from rafters of the barn we built
to a landscape we knew;
we two spent evenings listening
to his stories of the Pacific war.
None of us know it,
but he'll be gone
day after tomorrow, and this
is the last thing we'll do together.

A Moral Life

I couldn't help it. Others
were clearing brush. *O, why not join in.*
There'd be uneven ground, a guard rail to ignore.
I got immersed. My balloon went up in a lovely affair.

As the sun arcs past its horizon nadir,
the cabaret streets hold themselves open,
where citizens roam blankness
the stranded night evokes,
then return home, wondering
what the fuss was all about.
They are the others in my life, sometimes
teachers, sometimes villains.
In the end I get to decide.

What did it matter if I stumbled with weed sling in hand?
Doesn't the earth demand earthiness, earthliness,
prayers offered by tarnished hands?
Tomorrow I think I'll go back to clearing brush,
for the sake of those moments,
where I try to gain, and regain, possession of myself:
this play becomes the work of survival,
a kind of moral life.

Swan Dive

Look at me with these nouns, mounting verbs,
these lines somehow linking
like a novice on a balance beam,
gangly, unmeasured, trying to find a stance.
If only this language was more substantial.
If only I could make a life beyond this life,
one I didn't grow bored of.
Well, *Night-night.* Tomorrow I'll try again.

How many times does confusion back me up,
leaving me gut-punched and empty.
How often do my memories shimmer with heat,
making me think, after all the smoke
and flames, that something's been forged,
but what, I can't tell.

Once, I thought the pressure was on,
me trying to say what had been said before,
only better. Now, I've let myself off the hook.
I'll just play on paper, like the old days
at creek's bluff, leaping in abandon,
making my version of a swan dive.

Prairie Invitation

Sit with me on this roadside
while we write our names in the dust.

Never mind the gravel
under our rumps as we praise

all that roots in dark, silent earth,
see grasses pushed and bent

and raised again by wind,
enduring each season better than we.

Each now is a new now
teeming as every bladed leaf,

flower, and seed.
What you have

for understanding is as close
as the breeze on your cheek.

Feel the sun on your face
like an old friend's embrace.

Take your cues from each fly,
beetle, and bee, pollinate the day.

Oil Lamp

In midsummer shadows, it rests unlit,
its globe tapering to a clear glassy stovepipe,
like a neck supporting an upside-down head
housing the wick, whose brightness
may be adjusted using the handle,
poking like a lone broken ear from one side.
Below, a basin of oil
suggesting a halo the color of bourbon,
waits with purpose, withheld fire.

Most days I pass it without a thought,
like words I bear deep in memory,
but on stormy nights, when the co-op electricity
flickers the lights off, then on,
then off for good, I place it
squarely on the kitchen table
while darkness swirls outside,
and strike a match, hoping to light my way
through an hour of reading, and maybe
all the way through to enlightenment—
if the flame consents to last.

Saturday Night: Blanchard, Oklahoma

Inside the Baptist church,
hard on the blacktop highway:
men in short sleeves, and women

in cotton skirts plain as the soil,
sing under yellow bulb-light.
I can imagine myself standing with them,

somewhere between vestibule
and their clear-voiced faith—
though I'm only passing by

the hard-packed dirt parking lot—
Dodges, Fords, having found
a temporary space to park their desires.

Their alkaline voices
hold me, all of them standing,
all facing one direction,

all singing the words by heart.
Standing in that dusky air,
I hear my warmest tenor joining,

letting the highway ribbon away,
while I sing *I surrender all . . .*
a love song to buoy me in this dusk.

About the Author

Dale Cottingham is of mixed race, part Choctaw, part White. He has attended Bread Loaf, was a finalist in the 2021 Great Midwest Writing Contest, and won the 2019 New Millennium Award for poem of the year. He has published poems in many journals, including *Ploughshares* and the *Asheville Poetry Review,* as well as book reviews in *Rain Taxi* and other venues. He lives in Edmond, Oklahoma.